D1389624

Your beautiful Baby

With love from

Other books in this series:

Best Friends
Thank you Mum
Have a Perfect Day
My Dad, My Hero
I've got a crush on you
Stay Calm
Happy Birthday
My Sister
Beautiful Daughter

Published in 2013 by Helen Exley® Gifts in Great Britain. A copy of the CIP data is available from the British Library on request.
Printed in China.

12 11 10 9 8 7 6 5 4 3 2 1

ISBN: 978-1-84634-606-4

Published by HELEN EXLEY®
Helen Exley Gifts, 16 Chalk Hill, Watford, Herts WD19 4BG, UK.
www.helenexley.com

Your Beautiful Baby

WORDS AND ILLUSTRATIONS BY

JENNY KEMPE

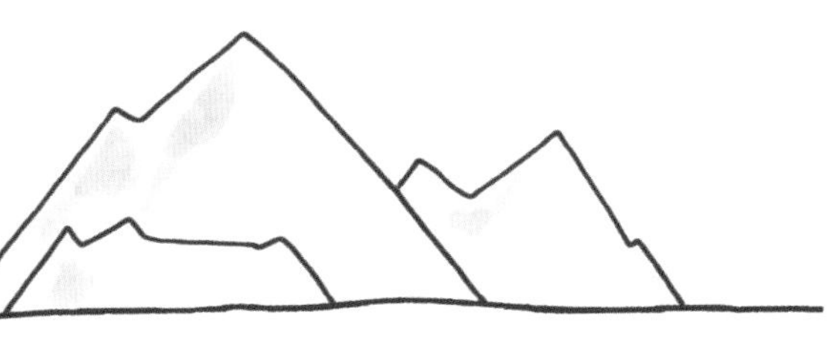

Knowing a little person
is on its way:
Hearts fill
with warmth
and an all encompassing
sense of JOY.

Preparing every little

etail.

Wondering what
Baby will be like.

Wondering who
Baby will be.

Waiting.

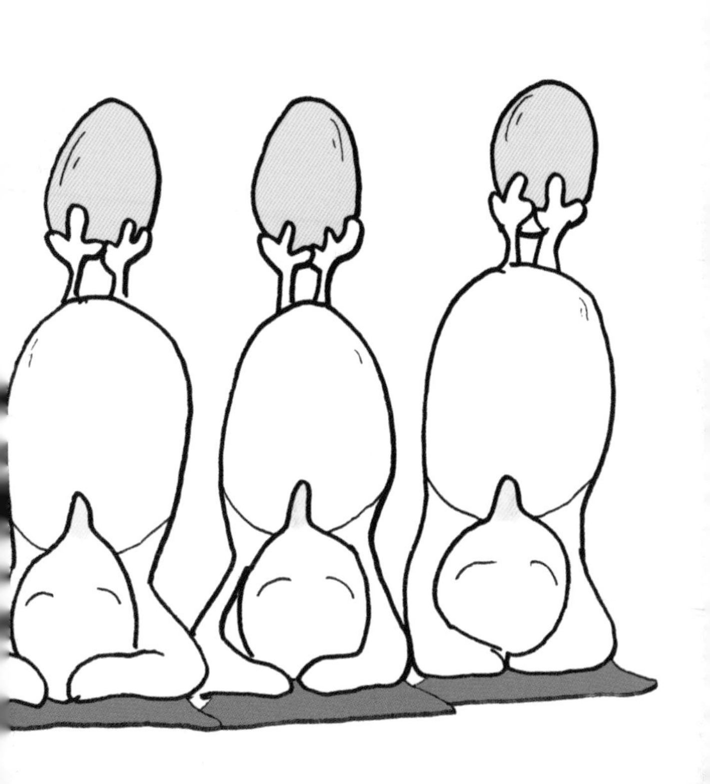

We all long to welcome your beautiful baby...

BABY
YOUR BEAUTIFUL BABY
JOY!

Seeing Baby

for the first time.

Falling in love again.

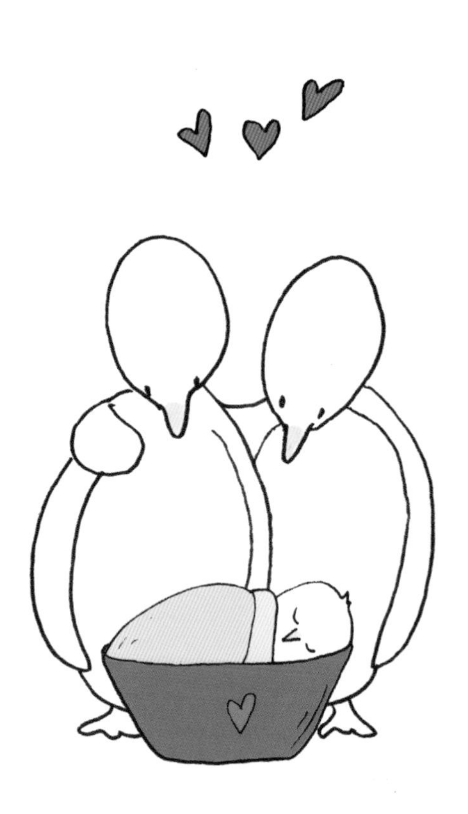

...lulling, soothing,
singing, dancing,
wishing, praying, begging,
just waiting for
the moment of sleep.

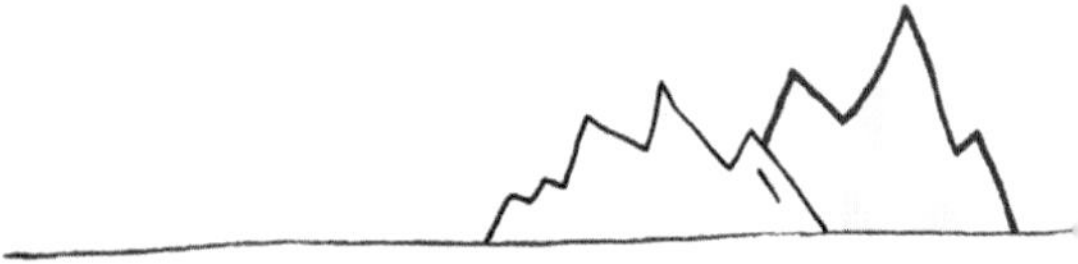

Feeling inadequate.

Finding strength.

Watching Baby grow.

0.5193

Hearing Baby

augh.

Caring, protecting.

Talking about your child.
Thinking about your child.
Every minute of the day.

Watching Baby.

Never, ever getting bored.

Feeling so proud.

Loving more tha

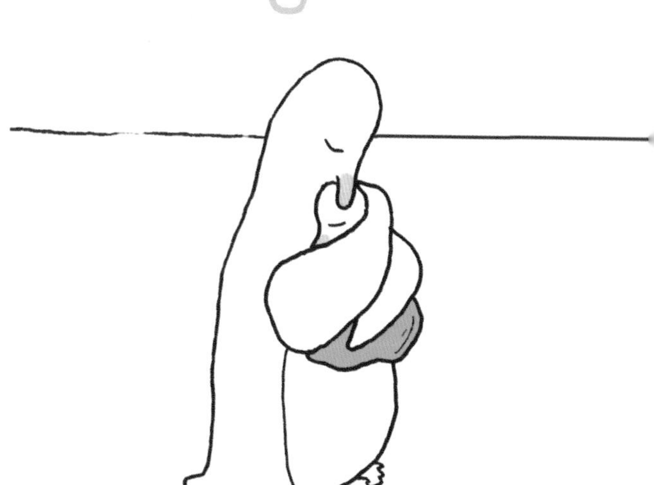

ever before.

Loving your beautiful little child
more than life itself...

Jenny Kempe

In 2009, overwhelmed by the endless bad news in the media, Jenny Kempe decided to take a six month break from newspapers, TV and radio. She turned her focus to the things in life that made her happy; to friends and family and to "taking time to just be". The result is the wonderfully bright and positive gift book series "Life is Beautiful". Each title has been designed to warm your heart and to put a smile on your face. As gifts, these books will brighten up the day, or even the life, of someone you care for.

www.jennykempe.com

We loved making this book for you.
We hope you'll enjoy the other titles
in our series Life is Beautiful.

The Life is Beautiful Team

About Helen Exley gifts

Our products cover the most powerful range of all human relationships: love between couples, the bonds within families and between friends. No expense is spared in making sure that each book is as thoughtful and meaningful a gift as it is possible to create: good to give, good to receive.
You have the result in your hands. If you have loved it – tell others!

Visit our website to see all of Helen Exley's other books and gifts: **www.helenexley.com**

Helen Exley Gifts
16 Chalk Hill, Watford, Herts
WD19 4BG, UK
www.helenexley.com